Index

- Finding the right investment strategies
- Learning to diversify investments

Chapter 6: Building a Passive Income Stream

- Exploring opportunities for passive income
- Creating a passive income portfolio
- Maximizing the potential of passive income

Chapter 7: Overcoming Financial Obstacles

- Identifying common financial obstacles
- Finding solutions to overcome financial obstacles
- Learning to stay motivated during financial challenges

Chapter 8: Achieving Financial Freedom

- Understanding what financial freedom means
- Creating a plan for financial freedom
- Living a fulfilling life with financial freedom

Chapter 9: Giving Back and Helping Others

- Understanding the importance of giving back
- Finding ways to help others with financial freedom
- Building a legacy of generosity

Chapter 10: Maintaining a Positive Money Mindset

- Learning to manage wealth wisely
- Staying motivated to achieve financial success
- Building a lifelong relationship with money.

Chapter 1: Understanding the Mindset for Money Gain

In order to gain financial success, it is important to have the right mindset. Many people hold limiting beliefs about money, such as the idea that it is scarce or that it is not possible for them to earn more. These beliefs can hold us back from taking action towards our financial goals.

To develop a positive money mindset, it is important to focus on abundance and to believe that money is readily available to us. This doesn't mean that we should be reckless with our finances, but rather that we should approach money with a sense of abundance rather than scarcity.

We can attract more money into our lives by visualizing our financial goals and taking action towards them. This might include learning new skills, starting a business, or exploring new career opportunities. It is also important to surround ourselves with positive influences, such as successful entrepreneurs or financial advisors, who can help us develop a mindset for financial success.

Identifying limiting beliefs about money

Identifying limiting beliefs about money is an important step in developing a positive money mindset. Limiting beliefs are beliefs that we hold that limit our potential for financial success.

Common limiting beliefs about money include:

- Money is the root of all evil
- Rich people are greedy and selfish
- Money is scarce and hard to come by
- I'm not good with money
- I don't deserve to be wealthy

To identify your own limiting beliefs about money, take some time to reflect on your thoughts and feelings about money. Notice any negative self-talk or limiting beliefs that come up. Write them down and examine them critically. Are these beliefs based on facts or are they just assumptions?

Once you have identified your limiting beliefs, you can work to reframe them into more positive and empowering beliefs. For example, instead of thinking "I'm not good with money," you could reframe it as "I am capable of learning how to manage my finances and become financially successful." By reframing your limiting beliefs, you can develop a more positive and abundant money mindset.

Building a positive mindset for abundance

Building a positive mindset for abundance involves developing a mindset that is focused on opportunities, growth, and positivity. Here are some tips for building a positive mindset for abundance:

1. Practice gratitude: Focus on what you have rather than what you lack. Take time each day to reflect on the things you are grateful for.
2. Focus on possibilities: Instead of dwelling on limitations or problems, focus on the opportunities that exist. Ask yourself: what can I do to improve my financial situation?

3. Visualize your success: Imagine yourself achieving your financial goals. Visualize the success you want to achieve and how it will make you feel.
4. Surround yourself with positivity: Spend time with people who have a positive outlook on life and are supportive of your financial goals. Avoid people who are negative or who bring you down.
5. Learn from failure: Failure is a part of the journey towards success. Instead of letting failure bring you down, use it as an opportunity to learn and grow.
6. Take action: Building a positive mindset for abundance is not just about thinking positively, it's also about taking action towards your goals. Take small steps each day towards your financial goals.

By developing a positive mindset for abundance, you can attract more opportunities and success into your life. With a positive mindset, you will be better equipped to overcome challenges and achieve financial success.

Learning to attract money with the right attitude

Learning to attract money with the right attitude involves developing a mindset of abundance and positive expectation. Here are some tips for attracting money with the right attitude:

1. Believe that money is abundant: Rather than believing that there is a limited amount of money available, believe that money is abundant and there is plenty of it available for everyone.
2. Focus on what you want: Instead of focusing on what you don't have, focus on what you want to achieve. Visualize yourself achieving your financial goals and believe that it is possible.

3. Take action: Attracting money requires taking action towards your goals. Take small steps each day towards achieving your financial goals.
4. Be open to receiving: Sometimes, we can unconsciously block ourselves from receiving money or abundance. Be open to receiving money and abundance into your life.
5. Use positive affirmations: Use positive affirmations to reinforce your belief in abundance and attract money into your life. Repeat affirmations such as "I am attracting wealth and abundance into my life" or "Money comes to me easily and effortlessly."
6. Practice gratitude: Gratitude is a powerful tool for attracting abundance into your life. Focus on what you have rather than what you lack, and express gratitude for the abundance in your life.

By developing the right attitude towards money, you can attract more money and abundance into your life. With the right mindset, you will be better equipped to achieve your financial goals and live a life of financial freedom.

Chapter 2: Developing a Plan for Financial Success

Developing a plan for financial success involves setting clear financial goals and creating a roadmap for achieving them. Here are some steps to develop a plan for financial success:

1. Define your financial goals: Begin by defining your financial goals. What do you want to achieve financially? Do you want to pay off debt, save for a down payment on a home, or invest for retirement? Make your goals specific, measurable, and time-bound.

2. Assess your current financial situation: In order to create a plan for financial success, you need to know where you stand financially. Take an inventory of your income, expenses, debt, and assets.
3. Create a budget: A budget is a powerful tool for managing your money and achieving your financial goals. Create a budget that accounts for your income, expenses, and savings goals.
4. Develop a plan to pay off debt: If you have debt, create a plan to pay it off as quickly as possible. Consider consolidating high-interest debt or exploring debt repayment strategies.
5. Save for emergencies: Building an emergency fund is a crucial part of any financial plan. Aim to save three to six months' worth of living expenses in an emergency fund.
6. Invest for the future: Investing is a key component of building long-term wealth. Explore different investment options, such as stocks, bonds, mutual funds, or real estate.
7. Monitor your progress: Regularly review your progress towards your financial goals and make adjustments as needed. Celebrate your successes along the way.

By developing a plan for financial success, you can take control of your finances and work towards achieving your financial goals. With a clear plan in place, you will be better equipped to make informed financial decisions and build a solid financial foundation for your future.

Setting financial goals

Setting financial goals is an important first step in developing a plan for financial success. Here are some tips for setting financial goals:

1. Make your goals specific: Instead of setting a general goal like "save more money", make your goals specific and measurable. For example, "save $5,000 for a down payment on a house by the end of the year".
2. Set short-term and long-term goals: Setting both short-term and long-term financial goals is important. Short-term goals might include paying off a credit card or saving for a vacation, while long-term goals might include saving for retirement or paying off a mortgage.
3. Prioritize your goals: If you have multiple financial goals, prioritize them based on their importance and urgency. This will help you focus your efforts and resources where they are needed most.
4. Make your goals realistic: While it's important to set ambitious goals, it's also important to make them realistic. Setting unattainable goals can be demotivating and lead to frustration.
5. Make your goals time-bound: Setting a timeline for achieving your goals can help you stay on track and measure your progress. For example, "pay off $10,000 in credit card debt in 18 months".
6. Write down your goals: Writing down your goals can make them feel more tangible and increase your commitment to achieving them.

By setting specific, measurable, and realistic financial goals, you can create a clear roadmap for achieving financial success. With a clear set of goals in place, you will be better equipped to make informed financial decisions and take action towards achieving your financial aspirations.

Creating a budget and sticking to it

Creating a budget is a crucial part of any financial plan, and sticking to it is equally important. Here are some tips for creating a budget and sticking to it:

1. Determine your income: Start by determining your total income. This includes your salary, any bonuses, side hustles, or any other sources of income.
2. Track your expenses: Track all of your expenses for a month to get an accurate understanding of where your money is going. This includes everything from rent and groceries to entertainment and discretionary spending.
3. Categorize your expenses: Once you have a good idea of your monthly expenses, categorize them into fixed and variable expenses. Fixed expenses include bills that are the same every month, such as rent or car payments. Variable expenses are those that can fluctuate each month, such as groceries or entertainment.
4. Set spending limits: Set spending limits for each category of expenses based on your income and financial goals. Be realistic and make adjustments as needed.
5. Monitor your spending: Keep track of your spending each month to make sure you are sticking to your budget. Use a budgeting app or spreadsheet to help you stay organized.
6. Make adjustments as needed: If you find that you are consistently overspending in a particular category, make adjustments to your budget to bring your spending in line with your goals.
7. Stay motivated: Sticking to a budget can be challenging, but staying motivated is key. Keep your financial goals in mind and celebrate your successes along the way.

By creating a budget and sticking to it, you can take control of your finances and work towards achieving your financial goals. With a clear understanding of your income and expenses, you will be better equipped to make informed financial decisions and build a solid financial foundation for your future.

Building an emergency fund

Building an emergency fund is an important part of any financial plan. Here are some tips for building an emergency fund:

1. Set a savings goal: Determine how much you need to save for an emergency fund. Aim to save at least three to six months' worth of living expenses. This should cover basic living expenses, such as rent, utilities, groceries, and other necessary expenses.
2. Make it a priority: Building an emergency fund should be a top priority. Make saving for emergencies a regular part of your budget.
3. Automate your savings: Set up an automatic transfer from your checking account to a savings account each month. This will help you build your emergency fund without having to think about it.
4. Look for ways to cut expenses: Finding ways to cut expenses can help you free up money to put towards your emergency fund. Look for areas where you can reduce spending, such as eating out less, cutting cable or streaming services, or finding cheaper alternatives for necessary expenses.
5. Use windfalls wisely: Use unexpected windfalls, such as tax refunds or bonuses, to boost your emergency fund.
6. Keep your emergency fund separate: Keep your emergency fund in a separate savings account, away from your regular checking or savings accounts. This will help you avoid the

temptation to dip into it for non-emergency expenses.

By building an emergency fund, you can protect yourself from unexpected financial emergencies and avoid having to rely on credit cards or loans in a time of need. With a solid emergency fund in place, you will be better prepared to weather unexpected financial storms and work towards achieving your financial goals.

Investing for the long-term

Investing for the long-term is an important strategy for building wealth and achieving your financial goals. Here are some tips for investing for the long-term:

1. Start early: The earlier you start investing, the more time your money has to grow. Even small contributions can add up over time.
2. Choose the right investment vehicles: Choose investments that align with your financial goals and risk tolerance. For long-term investing, consider low-cost index funds or exchange-traded funds (ETFs) that provide broad market exposure.
3. Diversify your investments: Diversification can help reduce risk and increase returns over the long-term. Spread your investments across different asset classes, such as stocks, bonds, and real estate, and across different regions or sectors.
4. Avoid market timing: Trying to time the market can be risky and difficult. Instead, focus on a long-term investment strategy that can help you weather short-term market fluctuations.
5. Invest regularly: Invest a set amount of money on a regular basis, such as monthly or quarterly, to take advantage of dollar-cost averaging. This

strategy helps reduce the impact of market volatility on your investments over time.
6. Rebalance your portfolio: Rebalance your portfolio periodically to maintain your desired asset allocation. This can help you stay on track with your long-term investment goals.
7. Stay disciplined: Avoid making impulsive decisions based on short-term market movements. Stick to your long-term investment plan and remain disciplined in your approach.

By investing for the long-term, you can take advantage of compound interest and the power of time to build wealth and achieve your financial goals. With a diversified portfolio and a disciplined investment strategy, you can stay on track and make the most of your investments over the long haul.

Chapter 3: Improving Income Streams

In addition to developing a positive money mindset and building a solid plan for financial success, increasing your income is an important component of achieving financial stability and freedom. Here are some ways to improve your income streams:

1. Invest in education and skills: Investing in education and skills can increase your earning potential over the long-term. Consider taking courses or pursuing certifications that can help you advance in your career or explore new opportunities.
2. Negotiate your salary: Negotiating your salary can help you earn more money in your current job. Research salary data for your position and experience level and prepare to make a compelling case for why you deserve a higher salary.

3. Start a side hustle: Starting a side hustle can provide additional income and help you explore your passions and interests. Consider starting a business, freelancing, or offering services on the side to increase your earning potential.
4. Rent out assets: Renting out assets, such as a spare room, car, or equipment, can provide additional income streams. Consider listing your assets on rental platforms to earn extra money.
5. Monetize hobbies and skills: If you have a particular hobby or skill, consider monetizing it. You can sell handmade goods, offer classes or workshops, or provide consulting services to earn extra income.
6. Invest in passive income streams: Passive income streams, such as rental properties, dividend-paying stocks, and investment funds, can provide a reliable source of income over the long-term.

By improving your income streams, you can increase your earning potential and achieve your financial goals more quickly. With a combination of active and passive income streams, you can diversify your income sources and create a stable and sustainable financial future.

Evaluating current income sources

Before you can improve your income streams, it's important to evaluate your current income sources. Here are some steps to help you assess your current income:

1. Make a list of your income sources: Start by making a list of all the ways you earn money, including your primary job, freelance work, rental income, or investment income.

2. Calculate your total income: Add up the total amount of money you earn from each income source to get your total income.

3. Analyze your income sources: Take a closer look at each of your income sources to evaluate their stability, potential for growth, and how much time and effort they require.

4. Identify opportunities for improvement: Consider ways you can improve your current income sources. For example, if you work in a job with limited earning potential, you may need to invest in additional education or skills to advance in your career. Alternatively, if you have spare time, you may want to explore side hustles or other opportunities to earn additional income.

5. Consider diversifying your income: Diversifying your income sources can help reduce your reliance on any one source of income and provide more stability over the long-term. Look for opportunities to invest in passive income streams, such as rental properties or dividend-paying stocks, in addition to your primary income sources.

By evaluating your current income sources, you can identify opportunities to increase your earning potential and achieve your financial goals more quickly. With a clear understanding of your income sources and the potential for growth, you can create a plan to improve your income streams and build a more secure financial future.

Exploring ways to increase income

Exploring ways to increase income is an important step in achieving financial success. Here are some ideas to consider:

1. Negotiate a raise: If you work a traditional job, negotiating a raise can be an effective way to increase your income. Make sure you have a clear understanding of your job responsibilities, and research salary data to determine a reasonable salary range for your position.
2. Take on additional responsibilities: Taking on additional responsibilities at work can also increase your earning potential. Consider volunteering for projects or tasks that are outside of your current job description to showcase your skills and value to your employer.
3. Freelance or consult: Freelancing or consulting can provide additional income and flexibility. Consider offering your skills and expertise on platforms such as Fiverr or Upwork, or offering consulting services to businesses or individuals.
4. Sell goods or services online: You can also sell goods or services online through platforms such as Etsy, Amazon, or your own e-commerce store. This can be a good way to monetize a hobby or skill.
5. Rent out assets: Renting out assets such as a spare room, car, or equipment can provide additional income. Consider listing your assets on rental platforms such as Airbnb or Turo.
6. Invest in stocks or real estate: Investing in stocks or real estate can provide long-term passive income. Consider investing in dividend-paying stocks or purchasing rental properties to generate passive income streams.

By exploring ways to increase your income, you can improve your financial stability and achieve your financial goals more quickly. Be creative and open-minded, and don't be afraid to try new things to find the best opportunities for you.

Finding additional income streams

Finding additional income streams is an important step in achieving financial success. Here are some ideas to consider:

1. Create a side hustle: A side hustle is a part-time business or job that can help you earn extra income. Consider leveraging your skills and hobbies to create a side hustle. For example, if you're a talented writer, you could offer writing services to individuals or businesses.
2. Participate in the sharing economy: The sharing economy offers many opportunities to earn extra income. For example, you can rent out a spare room on Airbnb, rent out your car on Turo, or deliver food with services like Uber Eats or DoorDash.
3. Participate in the gig economy: The gig economy provides a flexible way to earn extra income. Consider using apps like TaskRabbit or Gigwalk to find short-term gigs that fit your skills and schedule.
4. Sell items online: Selling items online can be a lucrative way to earn extra income. You can sell items you no longer need on eBay, Amazon, or Craigslist. Alternatively, you can create your own e-commerce store to sell items you've created.
5. Offer freelance services: Freelance services can be a great way to earn extra income. If you have skills in areas like writing, design, or programming, consider offering your services on platforms like Upwork or Freelancer.
6. Invest in rental properties or dividend-paying stocks: Investing in rental properties or dividend-paying stocks can provide a long-term passive income stream. Consider researching and investing in properties or stocks that fit your investment goals and risk tolerance.

By finding additional income streams, you can improve your financial stability and achieve your financial goals more quickly. Be creative and open-minded, and don't be afraid to try new things to find the best opportunities for you.

Chapter 4: Reducing Expenses

Reducing expenses is an essential part of achieving financial success. By cutting unnecessary expenses, you can free up more money to invest, save, or pay off debt. Here are some ways to reduce expenses:

1. Create a budget: Creating a budget is the first step in reducing expenses. A budget can help you understand where your money is going and identify areas where you can cut back.
2. Cut back on discretionary expenses: Discretionary expenses are non-essential expenses that you can cut back on. This may include eating out less, reducing your entertainment budget, or cutting back on subscription services.
3. Negotiate bills: Negotiating bills can help you reduce your monthly expenses. Consider negotiating your cable or internet bill, or asking your insurance provider for discounts.
4. Shop smarter: Shopping smarter can help you save money on essential expenses. Consider buying in bulk, using coupons or discount codes, and shopping during sales or clearance events.
5. Use energy-efficient appliances: Using energy-efficient appliances can help you save money on your utility bills. Consider replacing older appliances with newer, more energy-efficient models.
6. Consider downsizing: Downsizing your home or car can help you save money on expenses like rent, mortgage payments, and car payments.

Consider whether downsizing is a viable option for you.

By reducing your expenses, you can free up more money to achieve your financial goals. Remember to focus on the expenses that have the biggest impact on your budget, and don't be afraid to make changes to your spending habits to achieve financial success.

Identifying unnecessary expenses

Identifying unnecessary expenses is an essential part of reducing expenses and achieving financial success. Here are some steps to help you identify unnecessary expenses:

1. Review your bank and credit card statements: Go through your bank and credit card statements to identify any recurring expenses that are non-essential, such as subscriptions, memberships, or other services you don't use frequently.
2. Assess your entertainment expenses: Take a look at your entertainment expenses, including dining out, streaming services, or other leisure activities. Determine if you can cut back on these expenses or find less expensive alternatives.
3. Evaluate your transportation expenses: Evaluate your transportation expenses, including car payments, insurance, gas, and maintenance costs. Determine if you can reduce these costs by using public transportation, carpooling, or downsizing to a more fuel-efficient car.
4. Consider your housing expenses: Review your housing expenses, including rent or mortgage payments, utilities, and maintenance costs. Determine if you can reduce these costs by

downsizing to a smaller home or apartment or finding ways to reduce your energy usage.

5. Look for other ways to save: There may be other ways to save money that you haven't considered yet. For example, you can save money on groceries by buying in bulk or shopping at discount stores.

By identifying unnecessary expenses, you can make informed decisions about where to cut back and reduce your expenses. Remember to focus on the expenses that have the biggest impact on your budget, and don't be afraid to make changes to your spending habits to achieve financial success.

Finding ways to cut back on expenses

Finding ways to cut back on expenses is an essential part of achieving financial success. Here are some steps to help you cut back on your expenses:

1. Create a budget: Creating a budget is the first step in cutting back on expenses. A budget can help you understand where your money is going and identify areas where you can cut back.
2. Cut back on non-essential expenses: Non-essential expenses, such as dining out, subscriptions, or entertainment, can quickly add up. Consider cutting back on these expenses or finding less expensive alternatives.
3. Look for discounts and coupons: Look for discounts and coupons for items you need to purchase. There are many websites and apps that offer coupons and deals on groceries, dining out, and other expenses.
4. Negotiate bills: Negotiate your bills, such as cable or internet bills, to reduce your monthly

expenses. Contact your service provider and ask if they offer any discounts or promotions.

5. Shop smarter: Shop smarter by purchasing items on sale or clearance, buying in bulk, or purchasing generic or store-brand items instead of name-brand products.
6. Use energy-efficient appliances: Energy-efficient appliances can help you save money on utility bills. Consider replacing older appliances with newer, more energy-efficient models.
7. Consider downsizing: Downsizing your home or car can help you save money on expenses like rent, mortgage payments, and car payments. Consider whether downsizing is a viable option for you.

By cutting back on your expenses, you can free up more money to achieve your financial goals. Remember to focus on the expenses that have the biggest impact on your budget, and don't be afraid to make changes to your spending habits to achieve financial success.

Developing a frugal mindset

Developing a frugal mindset is an important step towards achieving financial success. Here are some steps to help you develop a frugal mindset:

1. Change your perspective on spending: Instead of seeing spending as a way to reward yourself, think of it as a means to an end. Prioritize your long-term goals over short-term gratification.
2. Cut back on unnecessary expenses: Cut back on expenses that are not essential, such as eating out, buying clothes you don't need, or expensive hobbies. Focus on what you need versus what you want.

3. Shop with intention: Before making a purchase, ask yourself if you really need the item and if it will add value to your life. Research prices and compare deals before making a purchase.
4. Learn to appreciate the simple things: Practice gratitude and appreciate the simple things in life. Enjoy free activities such as reading, spending time with family and friends, or going for a walk.
5. Save and invest for the future: Develop a habit of saving and investing your money for the future. Set up automatic contributions to a savings account or investment portfolio.
6. Learn new skills: Learning new skills can help you save money by doing things yourself instead of hiring someone else to do it for you. For example, you can learn to cook, fix your own car or repair things around your home.

By developing a frugal mindset, you can save money, reduce your expenses and achieve your financial goals. Remember to focus on the bigger picture and prioritize your long-term goals over short-term spending.

Chapter 5: Building Wealth through Saving and Investing

In this chapter, we will discuss the importance of saving and investing for building long-term wealth. Here are some steps to help you build wealth through saving and investing:

1. Start early: The earlier you start saving and investing, the more time your money has to grow. Make saving and investing a priority as soon as you can.
2. Set clear financial goals: Setting clear financial goals will help you stay focused and motivated.

Identify your long-term goals, such as retirement, and set specific savings and investment targets.
   3. Build an emergency fund: Having an emergency fund can help you avoid going into debt when unexpected expenses arise. Aim to save 3-6 months' worth of living expenses in your emergency fund.
   4. Maximize your retirement contributions: Take advantage of tax-advantaged retirement accounts, such as 401(k) or IRA, and aim to maximize your contributions each year.
   5. Diversify your investments: Diversifying your investments can help you manage risk and maximize returns. Consider investing in a mix of stocks, bonds, and other assets.
   6. Minimize fees: Fees can eat into your investment returns, so aim to minimize fees as much as possible. Look for low-cost index funds or exchange-traded funds (ETFs) and avoid actively managed funds with high fees.
   7. Stay the course: Investing is a long-term game, and it's important to stay the course and avoid reacting to short-term market fluctuations. Stick to your investment plan and avoid making emotional decisions.

By saving and investing for the long-term, you can build wealth and achieve financial security. Remember to start early, set clear goals, diversify your investments, and minimize fees. Stay committed to your investment plan, and you'll be on the path to long-term financial success.

Understanding the importance of saving and investing

Saving and investing are critical components of building wealth and achieving financial security. Here are some reasons why saving and investing are important:

1. Compound interest: Compound interest is the magic of investing. When you invest your money, you earn interest on your principal and on the interest earned in previous years. Over time, this compounding effect can significantly increase your returns.
2. Inflation: Inflation erodes the purchasing power of your money over time. By investing your money, you can potentially earn returns that outpace inflation and maintain your purchasing power.
3. Emergency fund: Having a savings account or emergency fund can help you avoid going into debt when unexpected expenses arise, such as medical bills or car repairs.
4. Retirement: Investing in a retirement account, such as a 401(k) or IRA, can help you save for retirement and ensure that you have enough money to support yourself in your later years.
5. Financial freedom: Saving and investing can help you achieve financial freedom and allow you to pursue your goals and dreams without worrying about money.
6. Wealth building: By consistently saving and investing over time, you can build wealth and create a strong financial foundation for yourself and your family.

By prioritizing saving and investing, you can build wealth, achieve financial security, and set yourself up for long-term financial success. Remember to start early, set clear financial goals, and stay the course, and you'll be on your way to financial freedom.

Finding the right investment strategies

Finding the right investment strategies depends on your individual financial situation, risk tolerance, and investment goals. Here are some investment strategies to consider:

1. Index funds and ETFs: Index funds and exchange-traded funds (ETFs) are low-cost investment vehicles that provide diversification and exposure to a broad range of stocks or bonds. These are a great option for those who want to passively invest in the market.
2. Individual stocks: Investing in individual stocks can be riskier than index funds or ETFs, but it can also offer potentially higher returns. Consider investing in companies with a strong track record, competitive advantage, and a solid business model.
3. Real estate: Investing in real estate can provide long-term income and appreciation potential. Consider investing in rental properties, REITs (Real Estate Investment Trusts), or crowdfunding platforms that allow you to invest in real estate with smaller amounts.
4. Bonds: Investing in bonds can provide stability to your investment portfolio, as they offer a fixed return and are generally less volatile than stocks.
5. Robo-advisors: Robo-advisors are automated investment platforms that use algorithms to create and manage a diversified investment portfolio. This is a great option for those who want to invest in the market but prefer a hands-off approach.

When choosing an investment strategy, it's important to consider your investment objectives, risk tolerance, and time horizon. Consult with a financial advisor or do your own research to determine which investment strategies are right for you. Remember, investing is a long-term game, so stay committed to your investment plan and avoid making emotional decisions based on short-term market fluctuations.

Learning to diversify investments

Diversifying your investments is a critical part of any successful investment strategy. Here are some tips to help you diversify your investments:

1. Spread your investments across asset classes: Consider investing in a mix of stocks, bonds, and real estate to spread your investments across different asset classes.
2. Invest in different industries: Within each asset class, consider investing in different industries, such as technology, healthcare, or energy. This can help you avoid overexposure to any single industry.
3. Consider international investments: Investing in international markets can provide additional diversification and potentially higher returns.
4. Use different investment vehicles: Consider investing in different types of investment vehicles, such as index funds, individual stocks, bonds, and real estate. This can help you achieve diversification across different investment types.
5. Rebalance your portfolio: Rebalancing your portfolio regularly can help you maintain your desired asset allocation and avoid overexposure to any one asset class.

Remember, diversification is important because it helps spread risk across different investments, which can help reduce the impact of any one investment's performance on your overall portfolio. By diversifying your investments, you can potentially achieve better returns and reduce the risk of losing money.

Chapter 6: Building a Passive Income Stream

Passive income is a type of income that is earned without actively working for it. Building a passive income stream can help you generate income even when you're not actively working. Here are some ways to build a passive income stream:

1. Real estate investing: Investing in rental properties or real estate crowdfunding can provide a steady stream of rental income.
2. Dividend-paying stocks: Investing in dividend-paying stocks can provide a source of passive income in the form of regular dividend payments.
3. Peer-to-peer lending: Lending money through peer-to-peer platforms can generate passive income through interest payments.
4. Building a business: Creating a successful business can provide passive income through sales, royalties, or licensing agreements.
5. Creating digital products: Creating and selling digital products, such as eBooks, courses, or software, can generate passive income through sales.
6. Affiliate marketing: Promoting products or services through affiliate marketing can provide a source of passive income through commissions on sales.

When building a passive income stream, it's important to choose an option that aligns with your interests, skills, and financial goals. It's also important to do your research and assess the potential risks and rewards of each option before investing your time or money. Remember, building a passive income stream can take time and effort, but the rewards can be substantial in the long run.

Exploring opportunities for passive income

Here are some opportunities for passive income that you may want to explore:

1. Rental income: Owning rental properties can provide a steady stream of passive income from rent payments. You can choose to manage the properties yourself or hire a property manager to handle the day-to-day tasks.
2. Dividend-paying stocks: Investing in stocks that pay dividends can provide a source of passive income through regular dividend payments.
3. Real estate investment trusts (REITs): REITs are companies that own and operate income-producing real estate, such as apartment buildings, office spaces, or shopping centers. Investing in REITs can provide a passive source of rental income without owning a physical property.
4. Peer-to-peer lending: Lending money through peer-to-peer lending platforms can generate passive income through interest payments.
5. Digital products: Creating and selling digital products, such as eBooks, courses, or software, can generate passive income through sales.
6. Affiliate marketing: Promoting products or services through affiliate marketing can provide a source of passive income through commissions on sales.
7. Royalties: If you have a creative talent, such as writing, music, or art, you can earn passive income through royalties from the sale or licensing of your work.

Remember, when exploring opportunities for passive income, it's important to choose an option that aligns with your interests, skills, and financial goals. It's also important to do your research and assess the potential risks and rewards of each option before investing your time or money.

Creating a passive income portfolio

Creating a passive income portfolio can be a great way to generate income without actively working for it. Here are some steps to consider when building your passive income portfolio:

1. Determine your financial goals: Before you start building your portfolio, it's important to determine your financial goals. This will help you choose the right assets to include in your portfolio.
2. Choose your passive income streams: Evaluate the different passive income streams and choose the ones that align with your interests, skills, and financial goals. Consider diversifying your portfolio to reduce risk.
3. Calculate your income needs: Calculate the amount of income you need from your passive income streams to meet your financial goals. This will help you determine the amount of investment you need to make.
4. Create a budget: Develop a budget that includes your investment expenses and projected income. This will help you stay on track and ensure that you're not overspending.
5. Monitor your portfolio: Regularly monitor the performance of your passive income portfolio and make necessary adjustments. This will help you stay on track to meet your financial goals.
6. Be patient: Building a passive income portfolio takes time and effort. Be patient and focus on the long-term benefits of your portfolio.

Remember, building a passive income portfolio can be a great way to generate income without actively working for it, but it's important to do your research and assess the potential risks and rewards of each option before investing your time or money.

Maximizing the potential of passive income

Here are some ways to maximize the potential of passive income:

1. Diversify your portfolio: Diversifying your portfolio across different passive income streams can help reduce the risk of your income being affected by a single investment. Consider investing in a mix of real estate, stocks, bonds, and other income-producing assets.
2. Reinvest your earnings: Reinvesting your passive income earnings can help you grow your portfolio over time. You can use the earnings to purchase additional assets or reinvest in the same asset to compound your earnings.
3. Continuously learn and adapt: The world of passive income is constantly evolving, and it's important to stay informed about new opportunities, regulations, and trends. Continuously learning and adapting to changes in the market can help you maximize the potential of your passive income streams.
4. Leverage technology: With the rise of technology, there are now many platforms and tools available that can help you manage your passive income portfolio more efficiently. Consider using online investment platforms, robo-advisors, and other tools that can help you manage your portfolio and maximize your earnings.
5. Focus on long-term growth: Passive income streams can take time to build, and it's important to focus on long-term growth rather

than short-term gains. By focusing on long-term growth, you can ensure that your portfolio is sustainable and can continue to generate passive income for years to come.

Remember, maximizing the potential of passive income requires patience, discipline, and a willingness to learn and adapt. By following these tips and staying informed about new opportunities, you can build a passive income portfolio that can provide financial stability and freedom over the long-term.

Chapter 7: Overcoming Financial Obstacles

Financial obstacles can be a major challenge when it comes to achieving your financial goals. Here are some strategies for overcoming common financial obstacles:

1. High debt: If you have a significant amount of debt, consider creating a debt repayment plan to help you pay off your debts more quickly. You can also consider consolidating your debts into a single loan with a lower interest rate.
2. Low income: If you are struggling with a low income, consider exploring ways to increase your income, such as taking on a second job or starting a side business. You can also consider seeking out education or training to help you qualify for higher-paying jobs.
3. Lack of savings: If you don't have enough savings, consider creating a budget to help you save more money each month. You can also automate your savings by setting up automatic transfers from your checking account to your savings account.
4. Unexpected expenses: Unexpected expenses can quickly derail your financial plans. To prepare for these expenses, consider building an

emergency fund that can cover at least three to six months of living expenses.

5. Negative mindset: A negative mindset can make it difficult to achieve your financial goals. To overcome this obstacle, focus on developing a positive mindset and surrounding yourself with supportive people who can help you stay motivated.

Remember, overcoming financial obstacles takes time and effort. By developing a plan, taking action, and staying focused on your goals, you can overcome these obstacles and achieve financial success.

Identifying common financial obstacles

There are several common financial obstacles that can prevent people from achieving their financial goals. Here are some of the most common financial obstacles:

1. High debt: High levels of debt, such as credit card debt, student loans, or a mortgage, can make it difficult to achieve financial goals and save for the future.
2. Low income: Low wages or unstable income can make it difficult to save for the future or invest in income-generating assets.
3. Lack of savings: Without a solid emergency fund or savings account, unexpected expenses, such as a medical emergency or job loss, can derail financial plans.
4. Unexpected expenses: Unexpected expenses, such as car repairs or medical bills, can quickly eat into savings and make it difficult to stick to a budget.
5. Negative mindset: A negative mindset, such as feelings of hopelessness or a belief that financial success is out of reach, can prevent people from

taking positive steps toward achieving their financial goals.

6. Procrastination: Procrastination or a lack of action can prevent people from taking the necessary steps to achieve financial success, such as investing, budgeting, or building an emergency fund.

Identifying these common financial obstacles can help people develop a plan to overcome them and achieve financial success.

Finding solutions to overcome financial obstacles

Overcoming financial obstacles can be challenging, but there are many solutions to help you achieve your financial goals. Here are some strategies to overcome common financial obstacles:

1. High debt: One solution to overcome high debt is to create a debt repayment plan, such as the debt snowball or debt avalanche method, to pay off debts more quickly. You can also consider consolidating your debts into a single loan with a lower interest rate.
2. Low income: To overcome low income, consider finding ways to increase your income, such as taking on a second job, starting a side business, or seeking out education or training to qualify for higher-paying jobs.
3. Lack of savings: A solution to a lack of savings is to create a budget to help you save more money each month. You can also automate your savings by setting up automatic transfers from your checking account to your savings account.
4. Unexpected expenses: To prepare for unexpected expenses, consider building an emergency fund that can cover at least three to

six months of living expenses. You can also consider purchasing insurance, such as health or car insurance, to help mitigate unexpected expenses.

5. Negative mindset: A solution to a negative mindset is to focus on developing a positive mindset and surrounding yourself with supportive people who can help you stay motivated. You can also consider working with a financial planner or coach to help you develop a plan and stay on track.

6. Procrastination: To overcome procrastination, break down your financial goals into smaller, manageable steps and set deadlines for yourself. You can also find an accountability partner or join a community of like-minded individuals who are working toward similar financial goals.

Remember, overcoming financial obstacles takes time and effort, but with the right strategies and mindset, it is possible to achieve financial success.

Learning to stay motivated during financial challenges

Staying motivated during financial challenges can be difficult, but there are several strategies that can help you stay focused and on track:

1. Set realistic goals: Setting achievable financial goals is a great way to stay motivated. Break down larger goals into smaller, more manageable steps and set deadlines for each step.

2. Track your progress: Keep track of your progress toward your financial goals. This will help you see how far you've come and give you a sense of accomplishment.

3. Celebrate your successes: Celebrate your financial successes, no matter how small they may be. This will help keep you motivated and positive.
4. Find support: Seek support from family and friends who can offer encouragement and motivation. You can also join a financial support group or online community to connect with others who are going through similar challenges.
5. Focus on the big picture: When facing financial challenges, it can be easy to get bogged down in the day-to-day details. Try to stay focused on the big picture and remember why you are working toward your financial goals.
6. Learn from setbacks: Financial setbacks are inevitable, but it's important to learn from them and move forward. Use setbacks as an opportunity to reassess your strategy and make any necessary adjustments.

Remember that staying motivated during financial challenges takes effort and commitment. By setting realistic goals, tracking your progress, finding support, and staying focused on the big picture, you can overcome financial challenges and achieve your financial goals.

Chapter 8: Achieving Financial Freedom

Achieving financial freedom is the ultimate goal for many people, and it is possible with dedication and hard work. Here are some strategies for achieving financial freedom:

1. Live within your means: Spend less than you earn and avoid accumulating debt. This will help you maintain financial stability and give you the freedom to save and invest for your future.

2. Maximize your income: Find ways to increase your income, such as starting a side hustle or pursuing career advancement opportunities.
3. Invest for the long-term: Invest your money in a diversified portfolio that aligns with your risk tolerance and financial goals. Investing for the long-term can help you build wealth and achieve financial independence.
4. Create multiple income streams: In addition to your primary income, create multiple income streams through passive income or other sources. This can provide a safety net and help you achieve financial freedom faster.
5. Reduce expenses: Reduce unnecessary expenses and prioritize saving and investing. This will help you build a strong financial foundation and achieve your goals faster.
6. Focus on your mindset: Cultivate a positive mindset and develop healthy habits around money. This will help you stay motivated and committed to your financial goals.

Remember that achieving financial freedom is a journey, and it requires consistent effort and discipline. By living within your means, maximizing your income, investing for the long-term, creating multiple income streams, reducing expenses, and cultivating a positive mindset, you can achieve financial freedom and live the life you want.

Understanding what financial freedom means

Financial freedom means having enough money to cover all of your expenses, live the life you want, and achieve your financial goals without having to rely on a paycheck or anyone else. It means having the freedom to choose how you spend your time and money, rather than being limited by financial constraints.

Financial freedom is achieved when you have enough passive income or investments to cover your expenses, allowing you to have the freedom to work, travel, or pursue your interests without worrying about money. It means having the ability to retire comfortably, take time off work for personal or family reasons, or start a business or pursue a passion project.

For some people, financial freedom means living a frugal lifestyle, while for others it may mean having a luxurious lifestyle. The key is to determine what financial freedom means to you and create a plan to achieve it. Financial freedom is not a one-size-fits-all concept, and it requires different strategies and plans depending on individual goals and circumstances.

Creating a plan for financial freedom

Creating a plan for financial freedom involves several key steps. Here are some things to consider when creating your plan:

1. Set clear financial goals: Determine what financial freedom means to you and set clear goals to help you achieve it. Your goals should be specific, measurable, and achievable, and you should set a deadline for each one.
2. Assess your current financial situation: Determine your current income, expenses, debts, and assets. This will help you identify areas where you can reduce expenses, increase income, and invest your money.
3. Develop a budget: Create a budget to help you manage your expenses and prioritize saving and investing. Your budget should include all of your monthly expenses and identify areas where you can cut back on spending.
4. Reduce debt: Pay off any high-interest debt, such as credit card debt, as soon as possible.

This will help you save money on interest and free up more money to invest.

5. Increase income: Find ways to increase your income, such as starting a side business, pursuing career advancement opportunities, or investing in stocks or real estate.

6. Invest for the long-term: Invest your money in a diversified portfolio of stocks, bonds, and real estate that aligns with your risk tolerance and financial goals. This will help you build wealth and achieve financial independence over time.

7. Monitor and adjust your plan: Review your plan regularly and make adjustments as needed. Track your progress towards your goals and make changes as necessary to ensure that you stay on track.

Remember that achieving financial freedom is a journey, and it requires consistent effort and discipline. By setting clear financial goals, assessing your current situation, developing a budget, reducing debt, increasing income, investing for the long-term, and monitoring your plan, you can create a solid plan for achieving financial freedom.

Living a fulfilling life with financial freedom

Financial freedom is not just about accumulating wealth and having the ability to afford the things you want. It's also about living a fulfilling life where you have the freedom to pursue your passions, travel, spend time with loved ones, and give back to the community.

Here are some tips for living a fulfilling life with financial freedom:

1. Pursue your passions: Use your financial freedom to pursue hobbies and interests that you are passionate about. This could involve

traveling, taking classes, or starting a side business.

2. Give back to the community: Use your financial resources to make a positive impact on the world. This could involve volunteering, donating to charitable causes, or supporting social enterprises.
3. Build strong relationships: Use your financial freedom to invest in your relationships with family and friends. Spend quality time with loved ones and create meaningful memories together.
4. Take care of your health: Prioritize your physical and mental health by eating well, exercising regularly, and getting enough sleep. This will help you enjoy your financial freedom for years to come.
5. Maintain a work-life balance: Use your financial freedom to create a work-life balance that allows you to pursue your passions and spend time with loved ones. This may involve reducing your work hours or pursuing a more flexible work schedule.

By focusing on these key areas, you can live a fulfilling life with financial freedom. Remember that financial freedom is not just about accumulating wealth, but about using your resources to create a life that is meaningful and fulfilling for you and those around you.

Chapter 9: Giving Back and Helping Others

Once you have achieved financial success and freedom, it's important to consider giving back to the community and helping others. Not only is it a great way to make a positive impact, but it can also be incredibly fulfilling and rewarding.

Here are some tips for giving back and helping others:

1. Identify causes you care about: Think about the causes and organizations that you are passionate about. This could be anything from environmental conservation to social justice to education.
2. Volunteer your time: Find ways to volunteer your time and expertise to support these causes. This could involve mentoring, serving on a board, or helping with events or fundraising.
3. Donate to charitable causes: Consider making financial donations to charitable causes that align with your values. You can research organizations to ensure that your donations are being used effectively.
4. Support social enterprises: Look for businesses and organizations that are committed to making a positive social or environmental impact. By supporting these organizations, you can help create a more sustainable and equitable economy.
5. Encourage others to get involved: Spread the word about the causes and organizations you care about, and encourage others to get involved as well. This can help build a strong network of support and make an even greater impact.

Giving back and helping others is an important part of achieving financial success and freedom. By using your resources to make a positive impact, you can create a better world for yourself and those around you.

Understanding the importance of giving back

Giving back is an essential part of living a fulfilling life. While it is important to focus on your own financial success and well-being, it is equally important to use your resources to make a positive impact in the world. Here are some reasons why giving back is so important:

1. Makes a positive impact: Giving back allows you to make a positive impact in the world and to contribute to causes that you care about. This can help make the world a better place and improve the lives of others.
2. Fosters a sense of purpose: Helping others can give you a sense of purpose and fulfillment that comes from knowing that you are making a difference in the world.
3. Builds relationships: Volunteering and supporting causes can help you build relationships with like-minded people who share your values and interests.
4. Encourages gratitude: Giving back can also help you develop a sense of gratitude for the blessings in your own life. By helping others who are less fortunate, you can gain perspective on your own circumstances and feel grateful for what you have.
5. Sets an example: By giving back, you can set an example for others and inspire them to do the same. This can help create a ripple effect of positive change in the world.

Overall, giving back is an important part of living a fulfilling and meaningful life. It allows you to make a positive impact in the world, build relationships, and find a sense of purpose and fulfillment.

Finding ways to help others with financial freedom

Financial freedom provides the opportunity to help others in a variety of ways. Here are some ideas for using your resources to make a positive impact in the world:

1. Donate to a charity: Consider donating a portion of your income to a charity or nonprofit

organization that supports causes that you care about, such as education, poverty alleviation, or healthcare.

2. Volunteer: In addition to donating money, consider volunteering your time to a nonprofit or charity. This can be a great way to get involved in the community, meet like-minded people, and make a positive impact.

3. Mentorship: Consider mentoring someone who is less fortunate or who could benefit from your expertise. This could be someone who is just starting out in their career, or someone who needs guidance and support in achieving their goals.

4. Invest in socially responsible companies: Consider investing in companies that prioritize social responsibility and sustainability. This can help support businesses that are making a positive impact in the world.

5. Support small businesses: Consider supporting small businesses, particularly those owned by underrepresented groups, by shopping at local stores and restaurants or investing in small business loans.

Overall, there are many ways to use your financial freedom to help others. Whether you choose to donate to a charity, volunteer your time, mentor someone, or support socially responsible businesses, your contributions can make a significant impact in the world.

Building a legacy of generosity

Building a legacy of generosity involves not only giving back but also inspiring others to do the same. Here are some ways to build a legacy of generosity:

1. Lead by example: Set an example by living a generous life. This can include not only giving financially but also volunteering, mentoring, and supporting socially responsible businesses.
2. Share your story: Share your own experiences of how giving back has enriched your life and how it has impacted others. This can inspire others to get involved and make a difference.
3. Involve others: Involve your family, friends, and colleagues in your efforts to give back. This can include participating in volunteer activities together, supporting a common cause, or even organizing a charitable event.
4. Educate others: Educate others on the importance of giving back and the positive impact it can have. This can involve speaking at schools or community events, or simply sharing information on social media or through word of mouth.
5. Plan for the future: Consider including charitable giving in your estate plan to ensure that your legacy of generosity continues beyond your lifetime. This can include setting up a foundation or donating to a cause that you care about.

Building a legacy of generosity is not only a way to give back to the community, but also a way to inspire others to make a positive impact. By leading by example, sharing your story, involving others, educating others, and planning for the future, you can build a lasting legacy that will continue to make a difference for generations to come.

Chapter 10: Maintaining a Positive Money Mindset

Maintaining a positive money mindset is crucial to achieving financial success and overall well-being. Here are some ways to maintain a positive money mindset:

1. Practice gratitude: Take time to appreciate what you already have, including the money and resources that you have access to. This can help shift your focus from what you lack to what you have, creating a more positive outlook.
2. Focus on abundance: Believe that there is enough money and opportunities to go around. This can help you stay open to new opportunities and approaches that can help you achieve your financial goals.
3. Visualize success: Picture yourself achieving your financial goals and living the life you desire. Visualization can help motivate you and keep you focused on your goals.
4. Stay positive: Avoid negative self-talk and focus on the progress you have made rather than any setbacks or challenges. This can help you maintain a positive attitude and persevere through any difficulties.
5. Practice mindfulness: Take time to be present in the moment and tune out distractions. This can help you make better decisions, be more productive, and reduce stress.

By practicing gratitude, focusing on abundance, visualizing success, staying positive, and practicing mindfulness, you can maintain a positive money mindset that will help you achieve your financial goals and live a fulfilling life.

Learning to manage wealth wisely

Managing wealth wisely is essential to maintaining financial security and achieving long-term financial goals. Here are some ways to manage wealth wisely:

1. Create a financial plan: Develop a comprehensive financial plan that takes into account your current financial situation, long-term financial goals, and risk tolerance. This plan should include strategies for saving, investing, and managing debt.
2. Diversify investments: Diversifying investments can help reduce risk and maximize returns over the long term. This includes investing in a mix of asset classes such as stocks, bonds, and real estate, as well as diversifying within each asset class.
3. Manage debt: Avoid taking on excessive debt and manage any existing debt wisely by paying off high-interest debt first, negotiating lower interest rates, and consolidating debt when possible.
4. Rebalance investments: Regularly review and rebalance your investment portfolio to ensure that it aligns with your long-term goals and risk tolerance.
5. Stay informed: Stay up to date on financial news and trends that may affect your investments and financial planning strategies.
6. Seek professional advice: Consider working with a financial advisor who can provide personalized guidance and help you develop a customized wealth management plan.

By following these strategies, you can manage your wealth wisely and increase your chances of achieving long-term financial success.

Staying motivated to achieve financial success

Staying motivated to achieve financial success is essential, as it can take time and effort to reach your goals. Here are some ways to stay motivated:

1. Set specific and achievable goals: Break down your financial goals into specific, achievable

steps. This can help you stay focused and motivated as you work toward your goals.

2. Celebrate small wins: Celebrate each small milestone along the way to achieving your financial goals. This can help you stay motivated and committed to your plan.
3. Find accountability: Share your goals with a trusted friend, family member, or financial advisor who can provide support and hold you accountable.
4. Visualize success: Visualize yourself achieving your financial goals and imagine the sense of accomplishment you will feel. This can help you stay motivated and focused on your end goal.
5. Review your progress regularly: Regularly review your progress and make adjustments as needed. This can help you stay on track and avoid losing motivation due to setbacks or challenges.
6. Stay positive: Maintain a positive attitude and focus on the progress you have made rather than any setbacks or challenges. This can help you stay motivated and committed to your financial goals.

By staying motivated and committed to your financial goals, you can achieve financial success and create the life you desire.

Building a lifelong relationship with money.

Building a lifelong relationship with money involves developing a healthy attitude toward money and using it as a tool to achieve your goals and create a fulfilling life. Here are some tips for building a positive relationship with money:

1. Practice gratitude: Be grateful for what you have and focus on the positive aspects of your financial situation.
2. Educate yourself: Learn about personal finance and investing to make informed decisions about your money.
3. Develop a budget: Create a budget to track your expenses and ensure you are living within your means.
4. Save and invest: Develop a habit of saving and investing regularly to build long-term wealth.
5. Give back: Donate to charitable causes or give back to your community to create a sense of purpose and fulfillment.
6. Seek professional advice: Work with a financial advisor or other professionals to help you make sound financial decisions.
7. Avoid overspending: Avoid impulsive purchases and focus on needs rather than wants to avoid overspending.
8. Be mindful: Practice mindfulness when making financial decisions and be aware of how your choices impact your long-term financial goals.

By developing a positive relationship with money, you can use it as a tool to create a fulfilling and prosperous life for yourself and those around you.

"Thank You"

**Money Gain Mantra in Life – Book Copyright ©
2022 Ajay Gautam**